THE 39

Written by John Buchan

Retold by Andrew Lane

Illustrated by Ruth Palmer

Collins

CHAPTER 1

As I looked down at the body of Franklin Scudder, pinned to the floor of my flat by a long, thin knife, I wondered what exactly I'd got myself into. My life had seemed so simple just 12 hours before …

I think the first sign of the adventures to come was a story in the newspaper I read that morning on my way to work. It was the summer of 1914 and everyone knew that war was coming between England and Germany. But there was one person trying to stop the war and bring peace – the Greek Prime Minister, Mr Karolides.

I went to the theatre that night after work, and it was nearly midnight when I got back to my flat in central London. It was in a large mansion block called Portland Place, with a friendly chap on the door. I went up the stairs to my flat and turned the key in the door, but before I could go inside, someone was pushing past me, shoving me into the wall.

It was a small man with a thin beard and I recognised him as one of my neighbours who lived upstairs – an American named Scudder.

For a moment, I thought he was attacking me, but instead he rushed across to the window, and peered between the curtains.

He gestured to me to come in. I did, and he rushed back to the door and shut it. He put the chain across the door as well. I probably should've been worried, but he didn't seem dangerous. I was more amused at his actions than anything else.

"Mr Hannay, I need your help," he said, and peered out of the curtains again.

I walked across to my favourite armchair and sat down. "Tell me what you mean," I said.

He sat down opposite me and sighed. "I warn you, this is going to be difficult to believe," he started, staring at his hands. "Look, I'm a journalist. I came to Europe to write about the political situation – and find out if there really was going to be a war with Germany. As I interviewed more and more politicians and businessmen, I uncovered evidence of a secret organisation called the Black Stone that wanted the war to happen."

He glanced up at me, and I could see fear in his eyes. "You work in the City," he went on. "You must know that there are people who'd make a lot of money if there was a war by supplying weapons to both sides. The Black Stone's aim is to get England and Germany to fight and to destroy each other, using their weapons."

There was a noise outside, and he jumped.

"It's a cat," I said. "Don't worry."

"You've heard of the Greek Prime Minister, Mr Karolides?" he went on, leaning forward.

I nodded, thinking of the newspaper article I'd read earlier.

"He could spoil all their plans. He's an intelligent man, but he's also a *good* man. He's talking peace when other people are talking war, and he's being listened to. That's why a member of the Black Stone is going to kill him."

I felt a chill run through me. It was bizarre, sitting there in my flat and talking about a plot to assassinate a well-known politician. "How?" I asked urgently. "When?"

"I don't know *how*," he replied, "but I do know *when*. It's going to be on 17th June, when Mr Karolides is here in England for a peace conference. I discovered that if there's a war, when your British naval warships start to leave their home ports, they'll find German warships waiting for them, equipped with torpedoes and mines. You'll be wiped out."

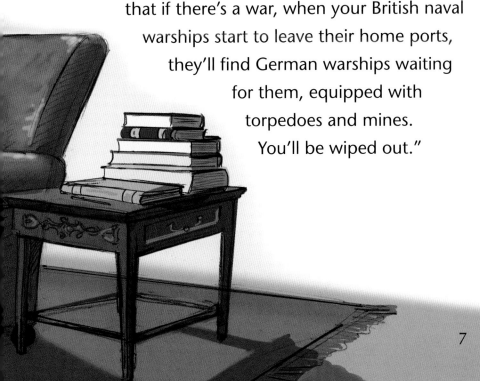

"But for that to happen," I pointed out, "the Germans would have to know where the ships are coming from, when they're leaving and what routes they'll be taking."

Scudder nodded. "The Black Stone intend stealing that information and passing it to the Germans."

"Can't you just *tell* someone?" I asked.

"I need to arrange some meetings with people I know in your government, but that might take time." He shook his head. "If the Black Stone find me they'll kill me, to stop me from exposing them. I thought I was safe here, but I was followed tonight. They know where I live." He looked at me pleadingly. "I need somewhere safe to stay – just for a few days."

I nodded reluctantly. "You can stay here," I said. "You can sleep on the sofa."

I left him scribbling in a little black notebook that night, and I headed for my bed. The next morning, I got up early. Scudder was curled up snoring under a blanket.

I spent all day in the City, wondering about his story, and I got back after sunset. I wanted to hear more about his plans for preventing the assassination of Mr Karolides. I even wanted to help.

That's when I found my guest lying on the floor with a knife in his chest. He'd been dead for a while.

CHAPTER 2

I felt sick, and had to sit down before I fainted, but staring at Scudder's white face didn't make me feel any better. Eventually, I had to cover his body with a tablecloth.

It was obvious now that Scudder's story was true, and that this mysterious group he'd talked about, Black Stone, had killed him so he couldn't stop their plan to assassinate Mr Karolides. It was also obvious that they'd kill me if they found me, on the basis that Scudder had probably told me everything. The only reason I wasn't dead now was that I'd been out all day.

I couldn't tell the police what had happened and ask for protection, because they'd immediately assume that *I* had murdered Scudder, and they'd arrest *me*. Even if I wasn't convicted, I wouldn't be in a position to prevent the assassination – and I knew that I had to try. I owed Scudder that much at least.

It was 24th May, and that meant I'd three weeks until the assassination was going to take place. I needed to get in touch with the government contacts that Scudder had talked about, but I didn't know who they were.

What I needed to do was to find a place of safety and work out what to do next – my flat wasn't safe.

I pulled the tablecloth off Scudder's body and carefully searched his pockets for the little black notebook he'd been writing in, but there was no sign of it. His killer must have taken it. I looked through a gap in the curtain, making sure there was no light behind me to give me away – but I couldn't see anyone watching the flat. I had to assume, however, that if I tried to leave then the Black Stone would know about it.

I sat in my armchair and waited until dawn. I tried to sleep, but the knowledge that there was a dead body by my side – and the body of a man I'd liked – meant that I stayed awake. That, of course, and the worry that Scudder's killer might come back for me.

In the end, I spent my time thinking about where to go while I worked out what to do, and I made up my mind to go to Scotland. My family had come from there, and in a strange way, it felt like home.

At five o'clock, I checked the train timetable I kept on a shelf. The next train to Edinburgh was at ten past seven, and I decided to catch it. In preparation, I put on one of my old tweed suits and a cloth cap from the back of the wardrobe.

By six o'clock, I was feeling hungry. I went to the kitchen to get some bread from the bread bin – but in it, next to the loaf, was Scudder's black notebook! He must have hidden it there, and the killer hadn't found it. That seemed like a good sign, and I felt more cheerful.

At twenty to seven, I heard the noise of the milkman outside. That was what I'd been waiting for. Quickly I sprang up from my chair and pulled open the door.

"I need your uniform!" I said.

He looked at me suspiciously. "Why?" he asked – quite reasonably.

"Fancy-dress party," I said. It was the first thing I could think of.

He just kept looking at me.

"There's money in it for you," I added. "I'll leave the uniform outside this door later on. You can come back for it."

He shrugged. "If there's money in it, I'll do it," he said.

I grabbed his coat and his cap, and set off down the stairs. As I got to the street, I looked casually left and right. A policeman was coming around the corner, and a tramp was just passing by. Apart from that, there was nobody about. The policeman didn't seem to be interested in my flat, but the tramp suddenly glanced over at a window of the building opposite. Looking up, I saw a face at the window. The face nodded at the tramp, who nodded back.

I felt a chill run through me as I realised that the flats *were* being watched, but I kept walking as if I didn't have a care in the world. Once past the milk cart and around the corner, however, I threw off the milkman's uniform and cap and started running.

I got to St Pancras Station at five past seven with
my heart feeling like it was going to burst. I jumped
the barrier, sprinted for the train while the guard
was blowing his whistle, and climbed on board just
as it started to move. Steam blew back into my eyes,
nearly blinding me. I found a seat just as the ticket
inspector arrived, and I bought a ticket for Wigtown –
the place where my family had once lived.
Strange, I thought, the way that life works out.

CHAPTER 3

It was a lovely day, and as the train steamed through the rolling English countryside, I found my spirits lifting. Then I remembered Scudder. He wouldn't be experiencing green fields or blue skies any more.

I was in a dark mood by the time we got to Crewe, but I managed to dash across the platform and buy a sandwich before the train left again. I didn't realise how hungry I was until I started to eat it, and then it was all I could do to stop myself wolfing it down in one go.

The food made me feel a bit better, and while the train headed towards Scotland, I took Scudder's notebook out of my pocket and began to read it. The pages were mostly filled with random, meaningless letters. Obviously it was some kind of code and I played with rearranging the letters for a while, trying to work out what they might mean, but I didn't get anywhere with it. Scudder was obviously a much cleverer man than I was.

I had to change trains at Dumfries, exchanging the fast train for a slow, rickety one that stopped at every station and was filled with local people – mostly men in hairy jackets, with whiskers, either going to market or returning from one. Most of the talk was about the prices they could get for their lambs or cows.

The landscape changed as we travelled. Through the grimy window, I could see hills and glens, crisscrossed with wide stretches of moorland and sparkling blue lakes.

I eventually got off the train at a station whose name I didn't even check. I only left because, for a few stations, the only people in my carriage who could have remembered me were asleep.

The station was a lone building on a white-edged road that headed into wild countryside in both directions. The air was cold, smelling of heather and peat, and the hills seemed diamond-sharp against the deep blue sky.

Despite the fact that Scudder's body would've been discovered by now, and I was probably wanted by the police, I felt freer than I had for a long time.

It was early evening, and despite my hunger, I set off along the road. Wearing my tweed suit, and unshaven, I didn't look out of place.

My plan – if you could call it a plan – was to walk to a station two or three stops up the line, and then catch a train heading south, back the way I'd come. If the police had managed to track me to St Pancras then they'd expect me to go as far as I could in the shortest possible time and they'd be checking the trains at the end of the line. If they *did* manage to work out I'd got off the train here, they might think I was hiding in some cottage; it wouldn't occur to them that I might double back on my tracks – I hoped. All I had to do, I kept telling myself, was to stay out of trouble until I could work out who to tell about the plot against Mr Karolides.

At last, I found a small station sheltering in a valley. It was so remote that it didn't even have a road leading to it or past it. I'd no idea what the timetable might be, but it was unlikely there'd be any trains until the morning. I didn't want anybody to see me hanging around the station, so I lay down in the heather and fell asleep.

I woke with a start. It was morning, and as I stiffly untangled myself from the heather, I heard the distant whistle of a train. I climbed to my feet, ran down to the station and jumped on the train as it arrived. I found a compartment where the only inhabitants were an elderly man with a bushy beard who was fast asleep and his cross-eyed dog, which watched my every move suspiciously. At least, I think it was watching my every move. It was difficult to tell.

There was a copy of the day's newspaper beside
the bearded sleeper, and I snatched it up to see
what news there was of Scudder's death. There was
a paragraph about it on page three with the heading:
"Portland Place Murder – brutal murder in a London
flat, milkman arrested and questioned but later released,
owner of the flat missing and sought by the police".
Worse, there was a photograph of me they must have
found in my flat. I folded the paper and put it back
with a sense of foreboding. I now knew that the hunt
was on.

CHAPTER 4

After a while, we arrived back at the same station where I'd got off the train the day before. I glanced out of the window, and immediately spotted three policemen who were questioning the ticket clerk. The train started up again just as he was pointing down the road, indicating the path I'd taken the day before. The police were cleverer than I'd thought – they'd catch up with me in no time unless I took action.

The train slowed to a halt at a crossing point in the countryside where a flock of sheep were milling about, and I saw a chance to escape unseen, rather than follow my original plan. I pulled down the window and looked along the length of the train. Nobody else was looking out, so I quickly opened the door and started to climb down. It would have worked perfectly if it hadn't been for the cross-eyed dog.

It suddenly started barking, waking up its master who began to shout. In panic, I jumped, leaving a scrap of my trousers behind in the dog's jaws, and sprinted for a thicket of bushes near the track. When I looked back, there were passengers looking out of every window to see what the fuss was about, and the guard had got off to see if there was a problem. After a while, when nobody could work out what had actually happened, the train started up again and pulled off.

My earlier good mood had vanished. Black thoughts sent me into a kind of blind panic, and I found myself running through the Scottish moorland, panting and sweating. I only stopped when I ran out of breath, and fell to the ground shivering. Gradually my breath, and my sanity, returned.

A buzzing up above me attracted my attention.
I glanced up – and immediately threw myself flat
on the ground. A small aeroplane was flying high in
the sky, and something told me that the people inside
were looking for me. I don't know *how* I knew that,
I just knew that the aircraft was a threat. I'd obviously
not been as clever as I'd thought about my escape.

I pulled heather and grass from the moorland and covered myself up, then watched without moving as the aeroplane circled for a while. In the end, it straightened out and flew away. I climbed to my feet and started to walk towards the distant road.

I walked for perhaps another hour until I found a small village with an inn. Over a decent dinner, I spent some more time with Scudder's notebook, trying to decipher the codes that he'd used, and surprisingly I managed to make a breakthrough. I knew that the name "Karolides" was important, so I wondered what would happen if I substituted the letters K-A-R-O-L-I-D-E and S for the most common letters in the English language – E-T-A-I-O-N-S-H and R. That proved to be the solution, but I realised that translating the whole notebook could take hours, so I went to bed, determined to do it in the morning.

I woke up abruptly at three o'clock in the morning when I heard a car pull up outside. I quickly dressed, and slipped out of my room. Listening from the balcony, I heard the door knocker bang loudly.

After a few minutes, the owner opened the door. Two men pushed past him and demanded to know whether he'd seen a tall Englishman in the past few days. The inn owner didn't like the way they were talking and demanded to know who they were. When they said they were policemen, he asked to see their identification. They refused, and he walked off, threatening to phone the real police. They followed, arguing.

While they were distracted, I crept downstairs, left the inn and stole their car. It was very thoughtful of them to leave the keys in the ignition.

I drove until the sun was well above the horizon, passing through several small villages and stopping in a town large enough for me to not stand out. Ravenously hungry, I found a café and sat down with a pot of tea, several slices of toast and Scudder's notebook. Within an hour, I'd translated the whole thing. It was pretty much as Scudder had explained to me, back in my flat, with the addition of some things he'd overheard somewhere and written down without understanding what they meant – things like "Black Stone will start the war", "There are 39 steps", "High tide is at 10:17 p.m.", and, most bizarrely, "Beware of the man who opens his eyes too wide – he's dangerous!" Fortunately for me, he'd also written down the name of the person in the British Government that he wanted to contact – Sir Walter Bullivant.

I left the café and set off again, driving through the Scottish countryside in my stolen car, down from the Highlands to the industrial landscape of the south.

After a while, I glanced up and I spotted the aircraft again in the sky, circling overhead. There was no doubt in my mind that it was the same aircraft as the day before, and it was still looking for me.

I took a side road towards a forest of pine trees, where the branches and leaves closed in above the car and shielded me as I drove.

There were patches of blue sky every now and then, when the car passed through a clearing in the trees, and every time I glanced up, I craned my neck to see if I could spot the aircraft.

It was on one of those occasions that I failed to spot a twist in the road. It went left, but I went straight on, ploughing into the forest and hitting a tree. The rest was darkness.

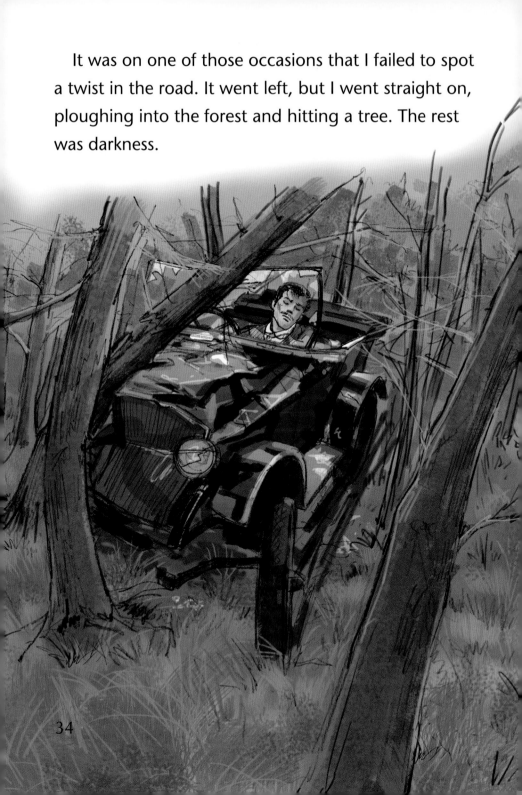

CHAPTER 5

I don't know how long I was unconscious but when I woke up there was blood in my hair and my head throbbed. It took me a while to get to my feet, but when I did I checked the car over. The good news was that it'd plunged far enough between the trees and into the undergrowth that it was invisible, both from the road and from the air. The bad news was that it was less of a car now and more like half a ton of useless metal.

Part of me just wanted to lie down again and sink back into unconsciousness for as long as I could, but another part of me – the annoyingly practical part – knew that I had to keep going. And so I walked slowly and painfully along the road, ready to leap into the bushes if I heard another car. Eventually, I reached the edge of the forest, and sat down for a rest.

The road ahead followed the land as it gradually descended towards a flat plain – a ribbon of white against the dark green, brown and purple. To my right were hills and to my left I could see dark mountains. Down on the plain, there was a single stone cottage with a thin trail of smoke coming out of its chimney.

I could hear birds calling to each other, and somewhere out of sight there was the rushing sound of a fast-moving stream.

Eventually, I stood up again and walked down the road towards the house. My intention had been to ask for some food and a bed for the night, as I had before, but I saw that there was an old, rusted bicycle propped up outside the front door. There was no sign of anybody around, so I took it, but I made a promise to myself to return it if I could.

I spent some time pedalling along the white stone road, stopping every now and then for a drink from the stream next to the road. I stopped at another isolated house and asked politely if I could buy some bread and some meat, but the woman who opened the door gave it to me for free. I'd forgotten about the kindly nature of the Scottish people.

I was in the middle of an isolated patch of moorland that stretched from horizon to horizon, when the aeroplane spotted me again. I hadn't heard it approach. The whirring of the bicycle's wheels and the clanking of its chains filled my ears and, stupidly, I was singing to keep my spirits up. It swooped low over me like some huge black bat, and I nearly steered off the road in surprise. The aircraft wheeled around ahead of me and circled back, and I could clearly make out a man looking down at me. I'd been discovered!

The pilot took the aircraft up again, and it headed off into the distance – presumably to report back to whoever had sent it out. I knew that the net would be closing around me soon. A roadblock would be set up ahead of me, for a start, and probably behind as well. The bicycle was no use to me now. I had to get off the road, so I threw it into a patch of gorse, where it would lie hidden, and I set off at right angles to the road, across the plain, on the side opposite the one where I'd dumped the bicycle.

After slogging through heather and gorse that kept catching my feet, I came to a slight ridge, a ripple in the ground that crossed the plain. Throwing myself down behind it for cover, I looked back.

Two cars had stopped on the road, nose to nose, and men had got out. They were advancing in my direction. I must have left a trail, and my trick with the bicycle hadn't thrown them off.

I scrambled through the gorse and heather, crouched low so that I was hidden by the ridge. I was in a panic – they knew where I was, and there'd be men closing in from all sides. And I knew what would happen to me when they found me.

Raising my head above the ridge, I noticed that the road I'd crawled away from curved back towards where I was hiding. On the side of the road was a pile of white rocks, and a massive hammer was leaning up against them.

Someone had been splitting the rocks to make stones to line the side of the road, but he'd vanished off somewhere – maybe to look for some food, maybe to sleep for a while.

It took me just a few minutes to take my jacket off, roll up my sleeves, dirty my face and hair, scuff up my boots, and then walk confidently out into the road, pick up the hammer and start smashing rocks as if I'd been doing it all my life.

I'd been working that way for 15 minutes when a car pulled up alongside me. There were two men in it, both smartly dressed. They eyed me suspiciously.

"Been here long?" the passenger asked.

I didn't even glance at him. "Aye," I said in my best Scottish accent. "Ten years this April workin' this road."

"Seen anyone you didn't know today?" he pressed.

"Aye," I said. "You."

The driver said something in a foreign language, and the passenger wound up his window. The car drove off. I watched it go, and I couldn't help but laugh. I'd outwitted them.

CHAPTER 6

Once the road was clear, I walked off back into
the heather, found a little dip, and curled up beneath
my jacket. I managed a fitful sleep, my stomach
knotting up with hunger and I awoke just after dawn,
stiff and starving. Standing up, I started to think about
where I might go to get some food in safety.

I walked along the road until I got to the nearest
village. I was confident that the men from the Black
Stone who wanted me dead were looking elsewhere
for me and were moving further and further away
by the minute, but in my tired and hungry state I'd
forgotten about my other pursuers – the police!

Their search was completely separate from that of the Black Stone, and I hadn't got more than a few metres into the village when a police car came down the road towards me.

The uniformed driver saw me, and skidded to a halt. "You!" he shouted. "Stop where you are!"

Three constables spilt out of the car and started moving towards me, faces grim. "Come along quietly!" one of them called. "Don't give us any trouble."

I ran.

There couldn't have been more than 20 or 30 houses in the village – solid stone constructions set in little gardens – and I kept running around corners out of sight of the police and then doubling back on myself, but they were wise to that kind of trick. Whenever I broke cover and crossed a space – a road, or a track or a gap between the houses – there was someone there to see me and raise the alarm.

Eventually, they managed to box me into a fenced-off area of common ground on the edge of the village. I sprinted across the ground, hearing them yelling behind me, heading for a gate in the fence. Beyond the gate was a copse of fir trees, and I had to summon up the last of my energy reserves to run through them and out of the other side.

I found myself on a gravelled driveway leading to an old house. I ran towards it, hoping in desperation that I could find somewhere to hide – a cellar, perhaps, a stable or a tool shed. I avoided the front door, heading around the side of the house, and ended up in a well-kept garden with a tall stone birdhouse at the far end.

There were French windows at the back of the house, and through them I saw an elderly man sitting at a desk, writing. He glanced up, saw me, and waved to me to come closer.

I was so tired, so disoriented, that I obeyed. He opened the French windows and beckoned me in. The room was dark, shadowed, and lit mainly by candles on the desk, by the light of which he'd been reading a pile of papers.

"I ... I was ... " I started to say in a Scottish accent, urgently trying to think of some believable reason why I'd turned up unexpectedly in his back garden. But he surprised me by gesturing to a chair and saying, "Please, Mr Hannay, sit down."

Stunned, I sank into the plush comfort of the chair.

"Catch your breath," he said. He was a plump man, dressed casually, with a bald head and a kind expression on his face. "I expect the police will be at the front door at any moment, asking if I've seen anything suspicious. I'll get rid of them."

He vanished through the door. For all I knew he'd gone to call the police in, but I couldn't run any further. I was exhausted. I was also amazed that he not only knew my name but didn't seem to care that the police were after me.

When he came back in and sat behind his desk, he was followed by a heavy-set man holding a gun, which he casually pointed at me. My stomach felt like the ground had suddenly vanished beneath my feet. I said, in the same Scottish accent I'd used before, "I think there's been some mistake – my name's not Hannay, it's Ainslie."

"Please," he said, "let's not argue over a name. I've been waiting for you. When I realised you were headed this way, I decided that I needed a base of operations nearby, and this house was empty, but I hardly expected you to walk right in." His eyes suddenly flickered, opening wide and then returning to normal. It was a strange little physical tic, and I went cold as I remembered Scudder's notebook, and the phrase: *Beware of the man who opens his eyes too wide – he's dangerous!*

"Please remove your jacket," he said. "I believe you may have a small notebook that I want."

"My name's not Hannay," I insisted, as I stood up and took my jacket off, as instructed, placing it over the back of the chair. "Maybe this Hannay owes you money or something – I don't care. I just want to leave here peacefully and go about my business."

He stared at me, and there was a cold, hateful and clever intelligence in those eyes. They fascinated me like the bright eyes of a snake.

"No," he said, "you *are* Richard Hannay."

I stepped towards the desk indignantly. The barrel of his bodyguard's revolver followed me.

"I'm not – " I said, and then swept my arm across the desk, knocking the candles on to his papers. They caught fire immediately, the flames flaring up in a bright curtain between us. The revolver fired, deafeningly, but by that time I was halfway across the room, heading for the French windows.

CHAPTER 7

Rather than run, which is what the old man would expect me to do, I hid on top of an old stone birdhouse. The entrances were big enough for birds but too small for me, but I managed to climb onto its flat roof, where I was hidden by a stone ledge. And there I passed out, overcome with tiredness and shock.

I awoke in bright sunshine, with my mouth so dry that my tongue was sticking to my cheek. My head was pounding. I've never felt as bad in my life as I did at that moment.

All was silence around me. I could smell smoke, and when I peered over the edge I could see that the library at the rear of the house had been gutted by fire. There was nobody in sight. When they couldn't find me, I suspect the men had left the house and regrouped elsewhere.

Once I was sure that the place was empty, I shakily climbed down. I had to get to Sir Walter Bullivant, I decided. No more trying to stay out of sight in Scotland – I had to go in search of the one man who might listen to me.

I walked away from the house and into the Scottish countryside. I was jacketless, my shirt was grey with smoke and there was a tear in my trousers, but fortunately my wallet was still in my pocket. I walked for miles, the fresh air clearing my head, and I drank, as I'd done before, from the clear streams that crossed the countryside. I picked apples from an orchard and took some bread from the basket of a baker's bicycle parked outside a shop in a village I walked through.

I eventually found an abandoned cottage whose roof had partially fallen in, and I stayed there for a while until my headache wore off. My jacket was still in the old man's possession, along with Scudder's notebook, but I remembered Sir Walter Bullivant's address in Berkshire and I was determined to head there regardless of what might happen.

I still had a pretty good idea of where the railway line was, and so I walked until my path crossed it, and then walked beside it until I found a station.

I must have looked more like a tramp than a normal traveller; the station master looked strangely at me when I produced my wallet and bought a ticket, but he didn't say anything apart from, "Have a good journey, now."

I had to change trains twice, alert for followers or watchers all the time. I looked so dirty no one would recognise me, but I found a discarded newspaper and kept my face hidden behind it, just in case. Eventually, I arrived at the nearest station to Sir Walter Bullivant's house.

I walked from the station, but stopped on a stone bridge over a river to think about how I was going to approach the man. What could I say that would prevent him from calling the police immediately?

As I stood there, looking down into the rushing water, a fisherman wearing untidy flannel trousers and jacket and carrying a fishing rod stopped beside me. Glancing sideways, I could see that he was middle-aged, with unkempt grey hair.

"Good afternoon," I said.

"Good afternoon," he responded. He pointed to a deep area of water near the point where a set of stone steps ran down from the bridge to a path by the river bank. "Do you see there? I swear there's a trout down there that's been dodging my hook for ten years now."

"I don't see him," I said, just being polite.

"He's there," the man said. "Looks like a black stone."

Black Stone! The organisation who were attempting to start the war!

"How many steps would you say there were running down from the bridge to the path?" he asked.

"I'd say there were ... 39 steps," I answered, remembering the phrase from Scudder's notebook.

"Quite right." He smiled, and extended his hand. "Mr Hannay, I believe. I've been hoping you'd make it here. I'm Sir Walter Bullivant."

I shook his hand warily, remembering the old man with the snake-like eyes. "How do you know who I am?" I asked.

"Mr Scudder had written to me, asking to see me on a matter of importance. He said that he'd identify himself in person with the words 'Black Stone', to which I'd respond, 'The 39 Steps'. It seemed very theatrical, but when his dead body was discovered, I started to take his letter more seriously. I saw in the newspaper that his body had been discovered in your flat, but unlike the police, I made the assumption that you were innocent, and that he'd been hiding there. I was hoping you might find your way to me, and I recognised you from your photograph in the newspaper. Now – you look half-starved. Let's get some food into you."

We went back to his large manor house, and I fell on dinner like a wolf. In between mouthfuls, I told him the whole story of my adventures. He listened impassively, nodding slightly every now and then.

"Let me make some calls," he said when I'd finished. "With luck, we can stop this whole affair in its tracks."

He was back in 20 minutes. I half-expected there to be a man holding a gun behind him, but he was alone, and his face was white.

"I've just been informed," he said in a strained tone of voice, "that Mr Karolides was shot dead an hour ago. Whoever the Black Stone are, they've obviously advanced their plans."

CHAPTER 8

I slept like the dead, and awoke the next morning to find Sir Walter at his desk in his study, reading telegrams. He hadn't slept.

"Ah, Hannay," he said, "sit yourself down. I've been communicating with the French Embassy. Their man, Vice-Admiral Royer, is now arriving sooner than planned to be briefed on our naval plans. I assume that the Black Stone will discover the change of plan, but they aren't going to be able to steal or even open Royer's briefcase to get the naval plans without us knowing, and if they kidnap him it will be obvious to us. We'll change where our boats are based, where they'll sail to and when, in the event of war – although that'll take some time and expense." He shook his head. "I'm sure they'll try something, but I can't see what."

"Their only hope," I pointed out, "is to somehow get the information without us knowing that they have it – that way we don't change our plans, and they can still destroy the fleet if there's a war."

"Royer will arrive tomorrow," he said. "He'll come straight to my house in London, where he'll be briefed by me, in the presence of the First Sea Lord. I'll be reading from a file which is classified Top Secret. After that, he'll be driven in an armed convoy straight to Portsmouth, where he'll board a French destroyer heading for Le Havre. He'll never be left alone."

"What about the Top Secret file?" I asked. "Someone will have to bring it *to* your house. Perhaps the Black Stone will strike then."

"The file will be in a locked briefcase and accompanied by armed soldiers." Sir Walter Bullivant sighed. "We should go to London. I suggest that you drive me, rather than my chauffeur. I want you close at hand."

We drove up after breakfast, and got to London by mid-morning. Waiting for us at Sir Walter's house was the chief constable of the Metropolitan Police.

"I've bought you the Portland Place murderer," Sir Walter said to him, but he smiled, and so did the chief constable.

"Mr Hannay," he said, shaking my hand. "I just wanted to tell you that you can take your life up where you left off. Mr Scudder's body has been removed from your flat, and you're under no suspicion. Sir Walter has told us everything."

I hung around Sir Walter's house, getting in the way of his butler, his footmen and his maids, while Sir Walter stayed in his study and made several phone calls. He had lunch delivered to his study and ate while he worked; I ate in the kitchen, getting in his cook's way as well.

Eventually, I wandered off, found a quiet room by the front door and waited to see what was going to happen.

At six o'clock, the doorbell rang and the butler admitted the Frenchman, Vice-Admiral Royer, along with his military escort. Sir Walter greeted him and escorted him to the dining room, which had been cleared for their meeting. The bodyguards remained outside.

At twenty past six the doorbell went again, and the butler showed in the First Sea Lord, with *his* military escort. I recognised him from photographs in the newspapers, of course, and Sir Walter greeted him like an old friend. He, too, was taken into the dining room.

An hour later, the dining room door opened and the First Sea Lord came out. Accompanied by his military escort, he walked towards the door, which the butler was opening. As he passed the doorway to the room in which I was waiting, he glanced sideways at me.

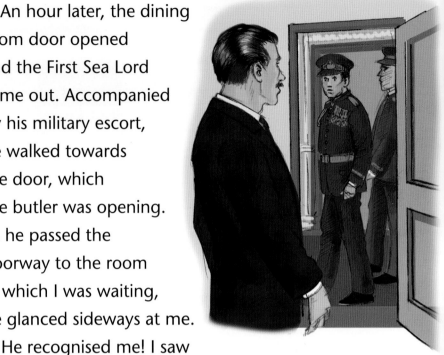

He recognised me! I saw it in his eyes – a slight flicker, and an expression of shock. It was momentary, but *I* knew that *he* knew who I was, even though we'd never met.

After he'd left, I ran for the dining room, past the French military escort, who tried to grab me, and burst in.

"Who was that who just left?" I shouted.

Sir Walter, who'd been talking to Vice-Admiral Royer, looked irritated at my interruption. "That was the First Sea Lord, Hannay," he said. "There's nothing to worry about."

"That *wasn't* the First Sea Lord," I exclaimed. "He knew me!"

Sir Walter stared at me for a long moment, and then went to a side table where a telephone rested. He dialled a number and spoke quietly for a while.

When he'd finished, he put the receiver down like a man handling delicate china. He turned to me and said, almost apologetically, "The First Sea Lord was taken ill earlier this afternoon. He's been in bed for hours. Whoever that man was, he was a *very* good imposter."

"He was working for the Black Stone," I said heavily, "and you've just briefed him on our top secret naval plans!"

CHAPTER 9

"He'll be in a fast car by now," Sir Walter said bitterly, "and he'll have changed his appearance. I'll send out instructions to change all our plans, but while that's happening, there'll be total confusion. The enemy might strike then!"

"Not necessarily," I said. "The imposter will need to deliver his plans in person. We can intercept him."

"But where?" Sir Walter asked.

I remembered another odd phrase from Scudder's notebook: *High tide is at 10:17 p.m.* "I believe Scudder knew the location of the handover," I said urgently. "We need to find somewhere where the high tide occurs at 10:17 p.m. on 17th June, when all of this was originally meant to happen."

"I'll get on to the admiralty," Sir Walter said. "They'll know, but there'll be many such places."

"It'll be isolated," I replied, "and a quick drive from London."

Sir Walter spent a while on the telephone, and then turned back to us. "There are several possibilities, but the most likely location is apparently a place called Ruff, in Kent."

He spoke again on the telephone, organising some kind of strike force, but I couldn't wait for him – time was critical.

I rushed outside. It was evening, and the very air seemed tense with anticipation. I jumped into Sir Walter's car and drove off as fast as I could, heading for Kent.

It took less than two hours. I parked the car near the beach, clambered down and walked until I could see the cliff and the villas perched on top. There were stairways coming down from each one, and I quickly counted the steps.

There was only one villa with 39 steps down to the beach.

I rushed over and started to climb up. Out at sea, I spotted a yacht. I couldn't help but think that it was a German ship, ready to take the information from the Black Stone. Time was desperately short.

The villa at the top of the stairs looked innocent enough. I cautiously walked around to the front, looking for anything out of the ordinary. Was I wrong?

I walked up to the front door and rang the bell. I had to know.

A young man with dark hair opened it.

"Could I speak to the owner?" I asked.

"Please," he said, "come in." As we passed through a hall with family photographs hanging in frames, he added, "We're just having a late dinner."

He led me into a candlelit dining room lined with more photographs, where two other men were sitting. One was in his thirties and quite plump, while the other was an older man wearing spectacles. When I saw him, I shivered. Was he the same man who'd threatened me in that house in Scotland – the one who had that strange trick with his eyes? I couldn't tell; his features were so bland, so ordinary, and the light was dim.

"Bob," the younger man said, "this chap says he needs to talk to you."

The older man stood up and smiled. "Bob Appleton. What can I do for you?"

I decided to push things a little further, to see what would happen. "This house is surrounded, and I have warrants for your arrest."

The older man stared at me, puzzled. "I'm sorry," he said, "but I don't understand."

The plump man looked genuinely confused. "Is this some kind of joke?"

"Arrest for *what*?" the younger man asked, stunned.

I couldn't tell whether they were genuinely surprised or great actors.

The older man frowned. "Look, I'm sure this is a misunderstanding. Why don't you take a seat, have a drink and we'll sort this out."

I looked around, desperately trying to spot anything in the room that was out of order or would give them away, but everything looked perfectly ordinary. Maybe I *had* made a mistake, and even now the secrets of the British naval plans were being passed to German agents on a different beach somewhere else in England.

The older man smiled gently at me, and gestured to me to take a seat. He got up and crossed to the drinks cabinet. His back was to me, but the candlelight caught his face and I could see his reflection in the glass of one of the framed photographs on the wall.

I saw his eyes suddenly open wide, and then close again as he blinked.

It was as if a veil had lifted. I saw him as he really was – the cold, malignant elderly man from the house in Scotland. I glanced at his companions, and their faces were now cold and ruthless where before they'd been friendly and puzzled. I thought I even recognised the young man as the one who'd disguised himself as the First Sea Lord.

The plump man suddenly pulled a gun out from beneath the table. As he pulled the trigger, I dived for the door. I felt the heat of the bullet as it passed my head. The younger man threw the candlesticks at me, plunging the room into darkness.

As I fell backwards into the hall, I saw the elderly man racing for a window that opened on to the garden.

The front door burst open and the police poured in. Within moments they'd grabbed the young man and his plump friend and were pulling them outside. I joined them, and saw that they'd caught the elderly man as well. He stared darkly at me as they pushed him into a police car.

Sir Walter Bullivant strode out of the darkness towards me. "We weren't sure where to go," he cried, "but then we heard the shot, and saw the lights go out. You've saved the country, Mr Hannay. Well done, man!"

Two weeks later, war finally broke out, but we were prepared for it. Two days after that, I joined the army, but I knew that my greatest service had already been performed, before I put on my uniform.

The Daily

No. 21,311   SUNDAY, MAY 24, 1914

PORTLAND PLACE MURDER

Brutal murder in a London flat, milkman arrested and questioned but later released, owner of the flat missing and sought by the police.

MAN ON THE RUN

A grisly sight met the police when they arrived at a flat in Portland Place, London. An American journalist, believed to be Mr Franklin Scudder, was found dead at the scene, with a knife in his chest.

Chronicle

ONE HALF PENNY

WANTED

The police are hunting the owner of the flat, Mr Richard Hannay, in connection with the murder of Mr Scudder. Mr Hannay left Portland Place just before 7 a.m. dressed in a milkman's uniform, and his whereabouts are currently unknown.

DISCOVERY

The police were alerted by the local milkman, who said Mr Richard Hannay owed him money and the return of his uniform.

CHARACTER

Neighbours living in Portland Place expressed their shock at the discovery. "Mr Scudder hadn't lived here long," one said. "He was a quiet man who kept to himself," said another. When asked about Mr Hannay, neighbours described him as an "ordinary chap" who worked in the City. As Mr Scudder's body was removed from the flat, a nationwide manhunt was launched for Richard Hannay.

Ideas for reading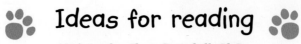

Written by Clare Dowdall, PhD
Lecturer and Primary Literacy Consultant

Reading objectives:
- ask questions to improve their understanding
- draw inferences such as inferring characters' feelings, thoughts and motives from their actions, and justify inferences with evidence
- summarise the main ideas drawn from more than one paragraph, identifying key details that support the main ideas
- identify how language, structure and presentation contribute to meaning

Spoken language objectives:
- participate in discussions, presentations, performances, role play, improvisations and debates

Curriculum links: History – British history; Computing – coding

Resources: ICT; pens and paper; map of UK

Build a context for reading

- Look at the front cover and read the title. Ask children to describe what they can see and to suggest what might be happening.
- Discuss when and where the story might be set and what we know about this time and place.
- Read the blurb aloud. Ask children to raise questions about the plot, e.g. *Why do the police suspect Richard Hannay of murder? What sort of organisation is the Black Stone?* Keep a note of the questions raised.

Understand and apply reading strategies

- Ask children to read Chapter 1 silently, and to be ready to summarise and recount the facts presented as a group.
- Work together to create a visual overview of the story opening that includes key people, events and information. Explain how this helps to create a context for reading.